THE BEST OF
BRAIN WAVES

MATHS,
SCIENCE
AND
TECHNOLOGY

Key Stage 1

Specially produced for School Book Fairs Ltd.

Folens
COPYMASTER

First published 1991 by Folens Limited, Dunstable and Dublin.

ISBN 185276326-4

Folens Limited. Apex Business Centre, Boscombe Road, Dunstable, LU5 4RL, England.

Contents

BRAIN WAVES SCIENCE
Alan Ward

Teachers' notes	4
Name this clown	6
Are all people different?	7
Funny faces	8
On the level	9
Packing groceries	10
Model window	11
A week of weather	12
Push or pull	13
Pulling a face	14
Electrical things	15
Squeak up please!	16
Cat and mouse	17
Planet earth	18

BRAIN WAVES MATHS
*Elaine Baker, Brian Hillary, Chris Hillary,
Steve Noon, Patricia Ruff*

Teachers' notes	19
Funny faces	20-21
The gingerbread man game	22-23
Variations	24-25
Number jigsaw	26-27
Turn the card	28-29
Count a caterpillar	30-31
Animal magic	32

BRAIN WAVES TECHNOLOGY
*Elaine Baker, Brian Hillary, Chris Hillary,
Steve Noon, Patricia Ruff*

Teachers' notes	33
Teddy bear	34-35
Dragons	36-37
Moving shapes	38-39
Pull the other one	40-41
Keep it tidy	42-43
Feed the birds	44-45
Badge brigade	46-47
Skill card	48

SCIENCE

Brain Waves Science - is an essential resource of quick, safe and simple ideas to assist primary teachers who wish to integrate science activities into their day-to-day teaching. The activities it contains are lively, imaginative and upto date, often experimental, and involve children working singly or in groups. They will encourage children to share in discussions and promote concern for how science and technology affect the environment and the lives of other people.

With few exceptions, the activities are designed to take place within an hour, using the minimum of preparation and materials. In most cases, it will be quite appropriate for the pupils to use the reverse side of the photocopied sheets for further ideas.

The content of the activites is inspired by the Programme of Study for Key Stage 2 of the National Curriculum for England and Wales.

The style of the activites is inspired by the approach to teaching and learning science emphasised in the description of Attainment Target 1 (Exploration of Science):

"The activities should encourage the ability to:

i. plan, hypothesise and predict
ii. design and carry out investigations
iii. interpret results and findings
iv. draw inferences
v. communicate exploratory tasks and experiments."

Science in the National Curriculum. HMSO 1989.

NAME THIS CLOWN *AT3:*
You could begin by rehearsing the naming of body parts, by asking the children appropriate questions. Ask them what sorts of names they will choose for the clown. When they have finished, they can colour in the picture.

ARE ALL PEOPLE DIFFERENT? *AT4:*
Even so-called identical twins have minor physical differences. Their fingerprints will not be the same and their characters may vary a great deal. After identifying the identical twins in the picture as the two blond-haired boys, use the picture to pose questions that will exercise the children's powers of observation. For example, you could ask how many of the children are boys, are girls, are dark-haired, are light-haired, etc.

FUNNY FACES *AT4:*
Emphasise the diversity of possible faces. Discuss the "Identikits" used by police forces. The pieces can be left on a "discovery table" for the children to experiment with at various appropriate times.

ON THE LEVEL *AT6:*
The force of gravity (see AT 10) makes liquids settle and spread, to cover the lowermost parts of containers. This response to the force of gravity is an important property of liquids, and it gives them horizontal surfaces. It is often said that "water seeks its own level".

PACKING GROCERIES *AT6:*
Make sure that the children understand and can use the word "groceries". They will have watched adults packing them in bags at the supermarket. Ask which items should be packed first. Why? Finally, invite the children to use their knowledge when they imagine that they are packing the bag pictured on the project sheet. The "packed" bags can be cut out and mounted in a display.

MODEL WINDOW *AT6:*
Discuss the word "transparent" and ask for examples of transparent things. Many children use the word "see-through" in this context. Help the children to make up the window cards. The window card idea can be adapted as a greetings card.

SCIENCE

A WEEK OF WEATHER *AT9:*
Discuss what making a weather diary or record means. Explain the use of symbols on weather maps, to make them simpler and more easy to read at a glance. Let the children invent weather symbols for their charts. Use the charts with the children, to record a whole school week of weather. This activity can be repeated at different times of the year, and the charts be compared.

PUSH OR PULL *AT10:*
Push forces include knocking in a nail, playing the piano, using a stapler, and biting the food. Pull forces include undoing the zip, heaving on the fishing-line, picking up the litter, holding the taut dog-lead, opening the can of drink, and getting ready to shoot an arrow. It should be well understood that the child is picking up the litter and not throwing it away!

PULLING A FACE *AT10:*
Encourage the children to follow the instructions and give them some help when folding the mouth. Explain that pushes and pulls are forces. By applying forces, they get their funny face toys to work. Discuss familiar examples of forces, such as picking up a toy from the floor (pulling) or kicking a ball (pushing). Use the project sheet as a prototype of the funny face toy idea. They can adapt the idea in many ways, to make greetings cards of subjects such as gulping frogs and beak-snapping birds!

ELECTRICAL THINGS *AT11:*
Discuss the dangers of mains electricity. Batteries are usually safe, certainly in everyday use in torches, toys, electronic watches and pocket video games, but the batteries constitute hazardous waste when they are thrown away. Also, talk to the children about dangers associated with power lines and local electricity sub-stations. Never fly a kite near high-tension powerlines etc.

SQUEAK UP PLEASE! *AT14:*
Folding the paper before cutting out the pattern is intended to make it easier for the children to cut the hole in the squeaker toy. This is an activity to do towards the end of a morning or afternoon, as these toys are noisy! Introduce the project by discussing different ways in which sounds can be produced. They all involve something moving, shaking, moving to and fro or up and down at a steady rate. This is called the sound's frequency, but that is not a word to tell the children. The steady shaking is called vibration. The children will be able to feel vibrations while they are working the squeakers.

CAT AND MOUSE *AT16:*
Prepare for this activity the day before, so that the children can start to observe the paper cats' shadows soon after school starts. Three or four paper cats, observed by groups of children will probably be enough. You need a wide south-facing window. Adapt the activity to suit your local conditions. Predicting where the shadow of the cat will pounce on the mouse is fun, although you should say that, since the cat is only a shadow, the mouse will not be hurt. Ask the children to suggest why the shadow moves. The sun, that casts the shadow, appears to move across the sky. Warn the children never to look directly at the sun. Where is the sun in the morning? Where is it in the late afternoon or evening?

PLANET EARTH *AT16:*
Show the children a globe. Explain that people living on the other side of the Earth don't fall off because the great size of the Earth produces a force called gravity. When you jump, gravity always pulls you down. Perhaps you can obtain a large colour photograph of the Earth, taken from a spacecraft. Ask the children what they think the colours mean.

Name This Clown

You need
pencil and paper
crayons

The name of my clown is [ ]

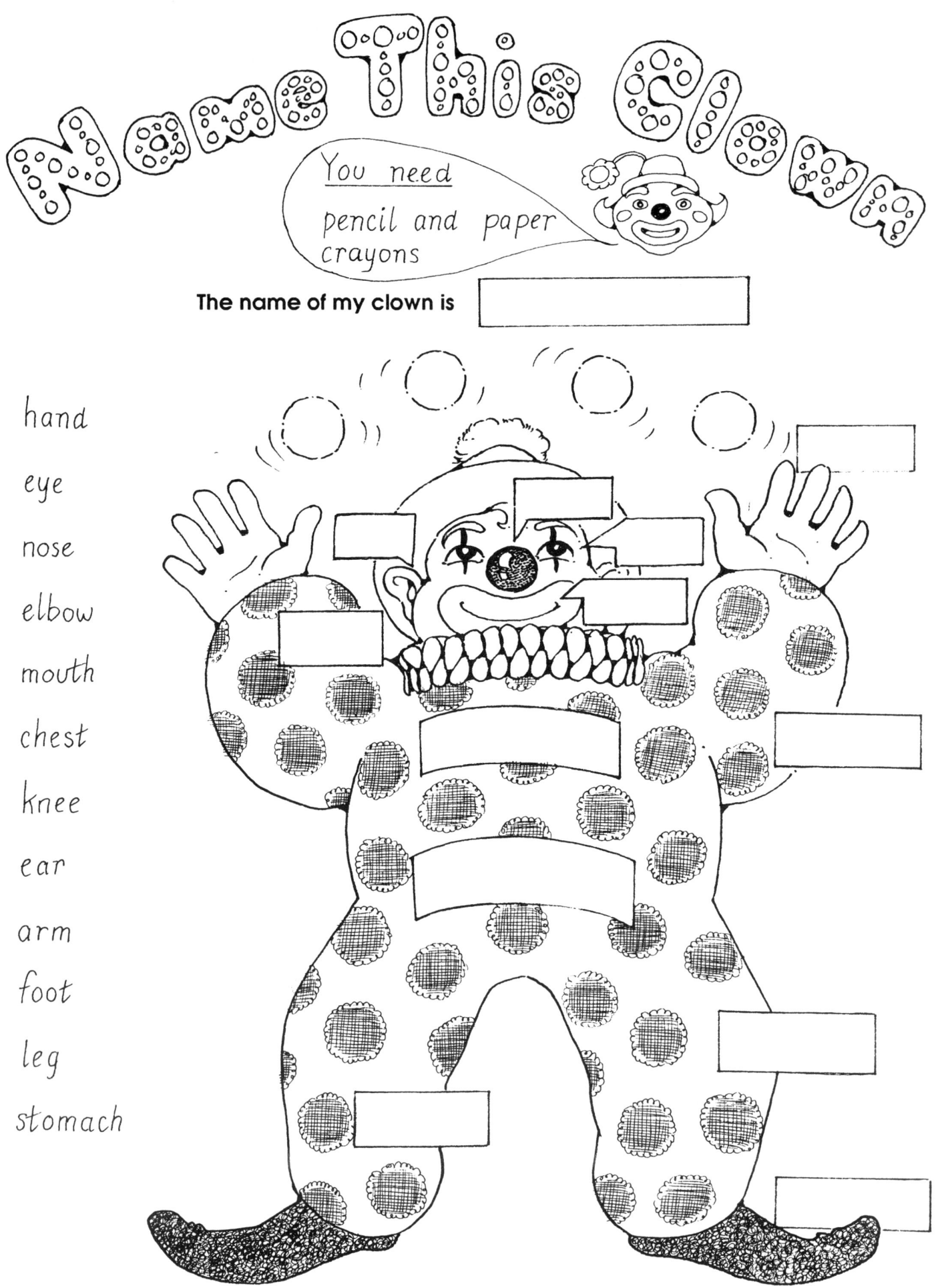

hand
eye
nose
elbow
mouth
chest
knee
ear
arm
foot
leg
stomach

Write the names of the parts of the clown's body in the right boxes.

Are All People Different?

Here is a class of children.
Can you spot the children that look the
same? We call them identical twins.

Draw 2 rings around the
identical twin children.

I can tell that the two children are identical because ....

_____

_____

_____

_____

FUNNY FACES

You need
pencil and paper
crayons
safe scissors.

Draw hair on this part of the face.

Draw eyes, nose and ears on this part.

Draw a mouth on this part.

Cut out the 3 pieces of your face.

Mix them up with the pieces that other children have made.

How many different funny faces can you make?

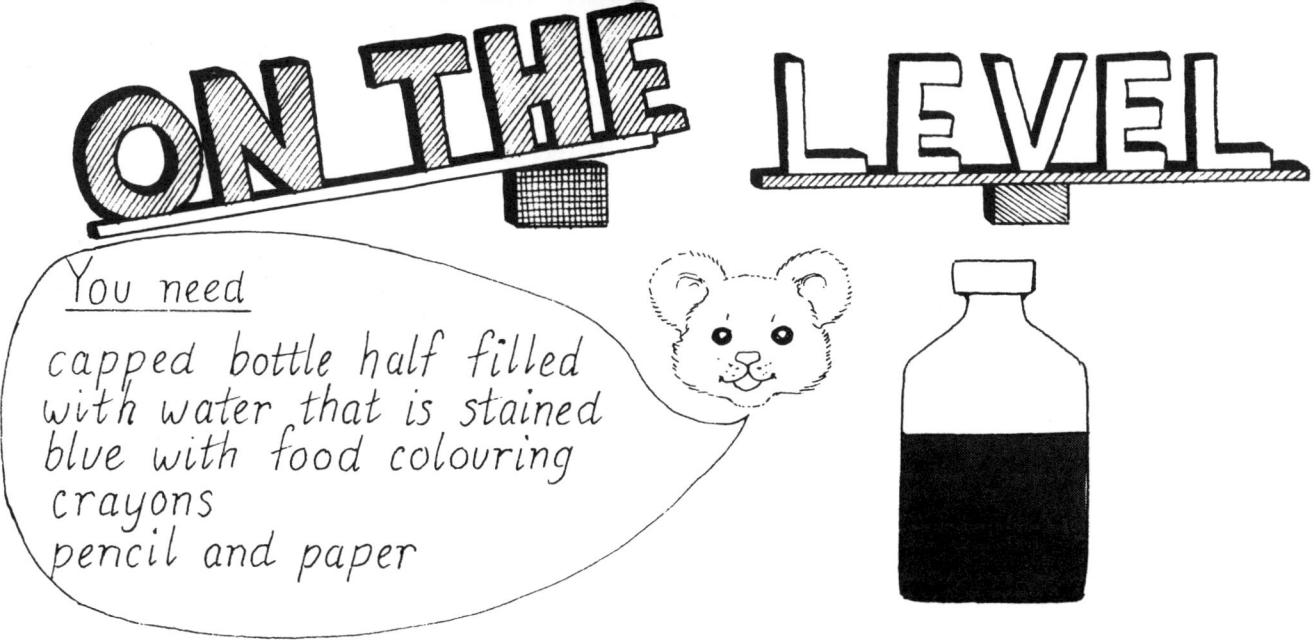

ON THE LEVEL

You need

capped bottle half filled with water that is stained blue with food colouring
crayons
pencil and paper

Here are some ways to hold the bottle of water.

Use the bottle you have been given to see what happens to the level of the water.

Draw blue lines on the bottle pictures to show the water levels.
Colour the water in the bottles blue.

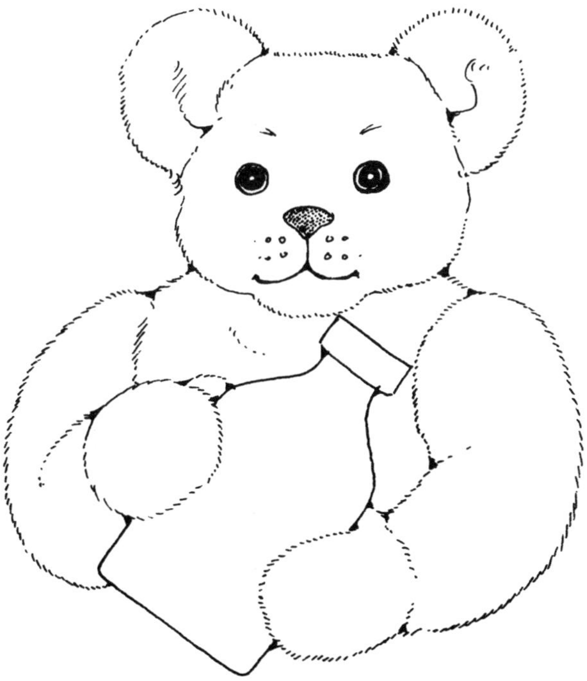

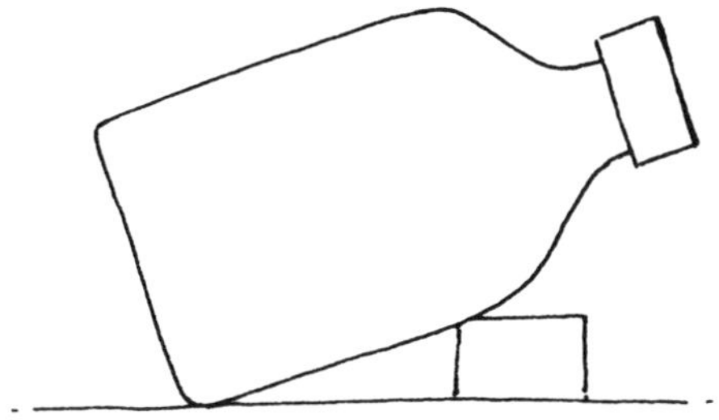

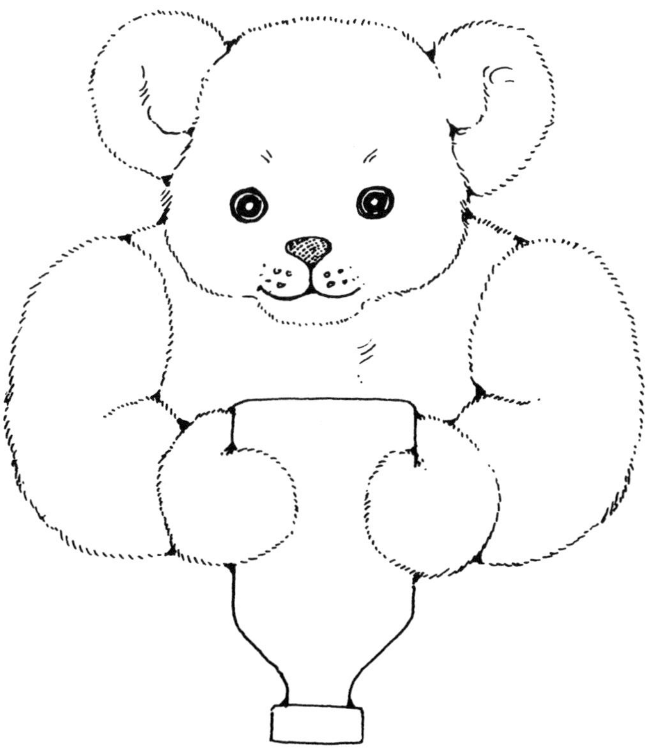

Why does the water stop moving where it does?

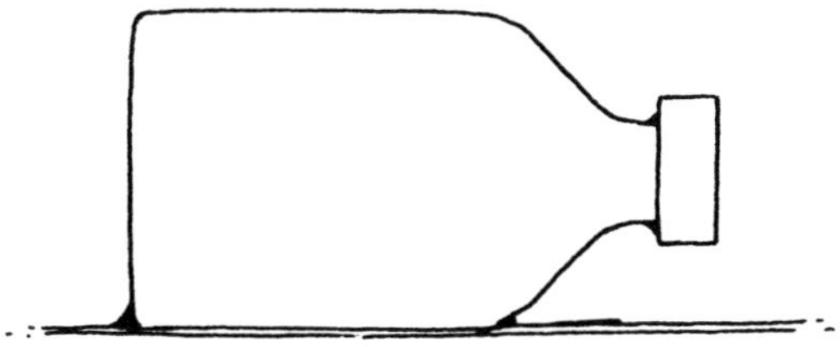

PACKING GROCERIES

You need

pencil and paper
safe scissors
glue and spreader

How should you pack these groceries in the bag?

Some must go in the bottom.
Some must go in the middle.
Some must go on top.

Tell your friends why the groceries should go in different parts of the bag.

Cut out the grocery pictures.

Glue the grocery pictures inside the bag.

MODEL WINDOW

"Transparent" means clear, or see-through.

These things are transparent:

bubbles   tap-water   air

Can you think of any others?

Cut along this line

Make a window here.

Cut out the opening.

Tape transparent plastic under it.

Write the names of some transparent things so that you can see them through your window.

fold here

Fold this side back, like a birthday card.

A WEEK OF WEATHER

You need pencils and paper crayons

Fill in a weather diary. Do it twice a day for a whole school week.

This is a weather symbol that means "sunny".

Make up your own symbols for different sort of weather.

Draw one symbol for the morning and one for the afternoon.

rainy	snowy	windy
cloudy	foggy	

My weather diary

Name [ ]

Write the dates under here	Days	Morning weather (draw your symbols)	Afternoon weather (draw your symbols)
	Monday		
	Tuesday		
	Wednesday		
	Thursday		
	Friday		

PUSH or PULL

You need pencil and paper

The pictures show pushing and pulling.

Write "push" or "pull" next to each picture.

PULLING A FACE

You need

pencil and paper
crayons
safe scissors
a little help from your teacher.

Here's how to make a funny face with a mouth that opens and shuts.

Draw and colour a funny face.

Cut a slit for the mouth.

Fold the paper to make a shape like a birthday card.
Fold back the edges.
When you close the shape, pull open the lips of the mouth and squash them flat.

How can you make the mouth open and close?

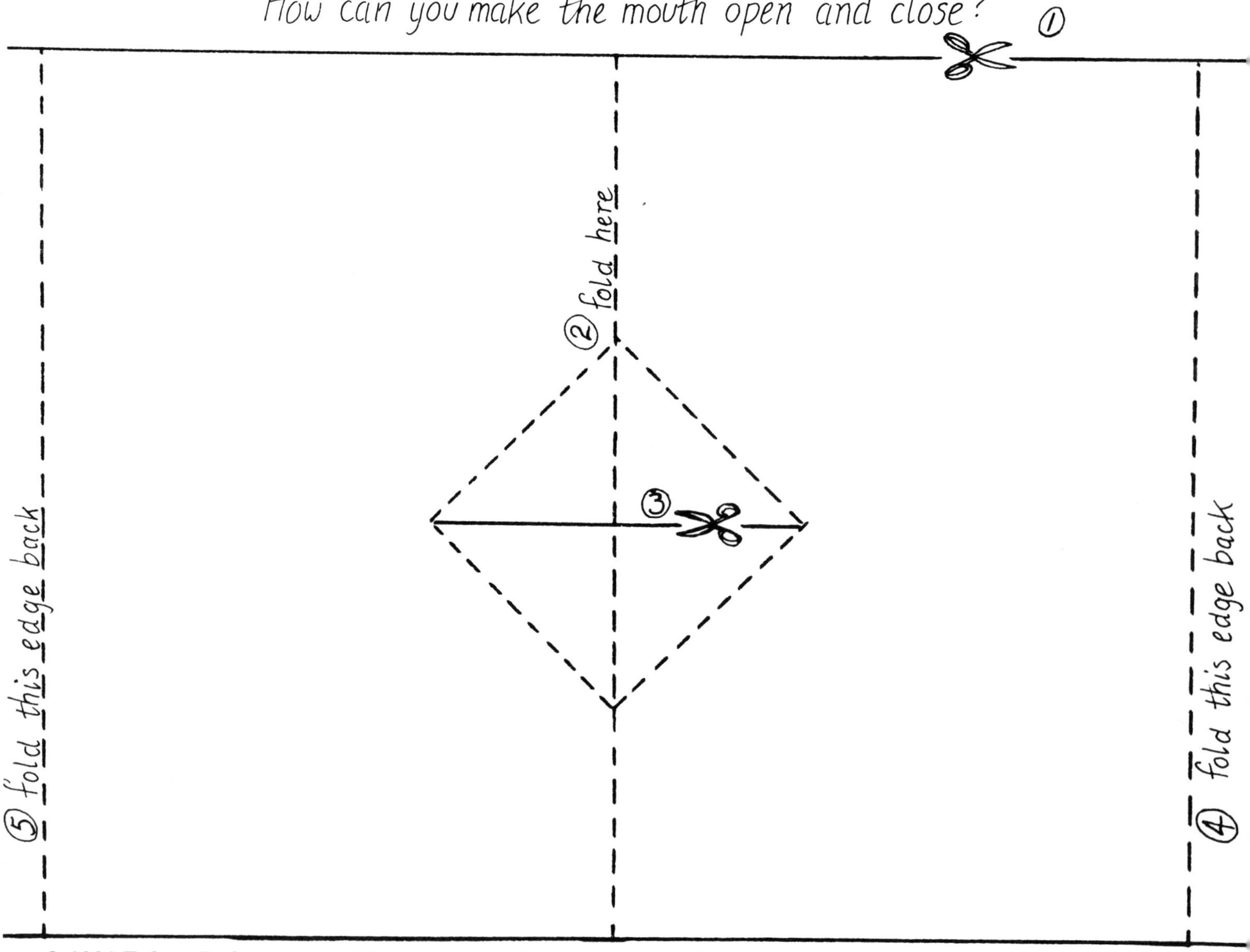

① ✂

⑤ fold this edge back

② fold here

③ ✂

④ fold this edge back

ELECTRICAL THINGS

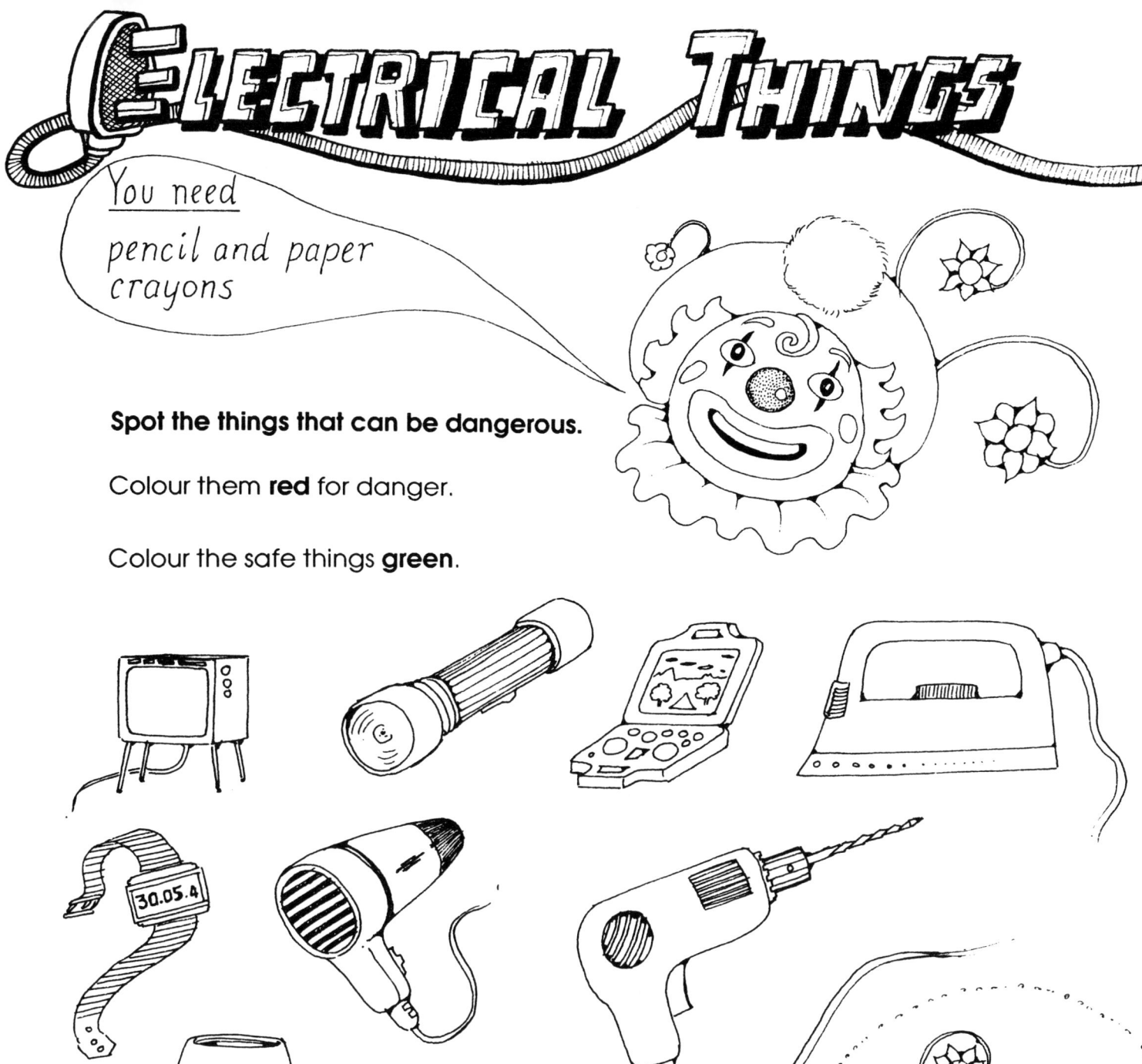

You need

pencil and paper
crayons

Spot the things that can be dangerous.

Colour them **red** for danger.

Colour the safe things **green**.

30.05.4

Here's
Billy...

He may look silly . . . but he
never touches electric wires
and plugs.

SQUEAK UP PLEASE !

You need
pencil and paper
safe scissors
crayons

You can cut out this toy and make it squeak.

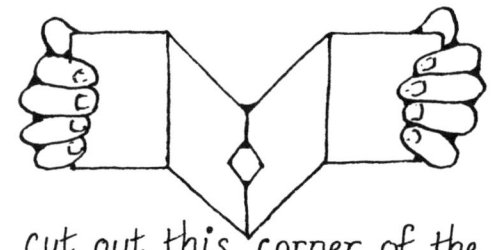

① cut out this corner of the sheet

Hold it like this.

Blow hard.

Listen to the loud noise.

Can you feel the paper shake?

You can feel **vibrations**.

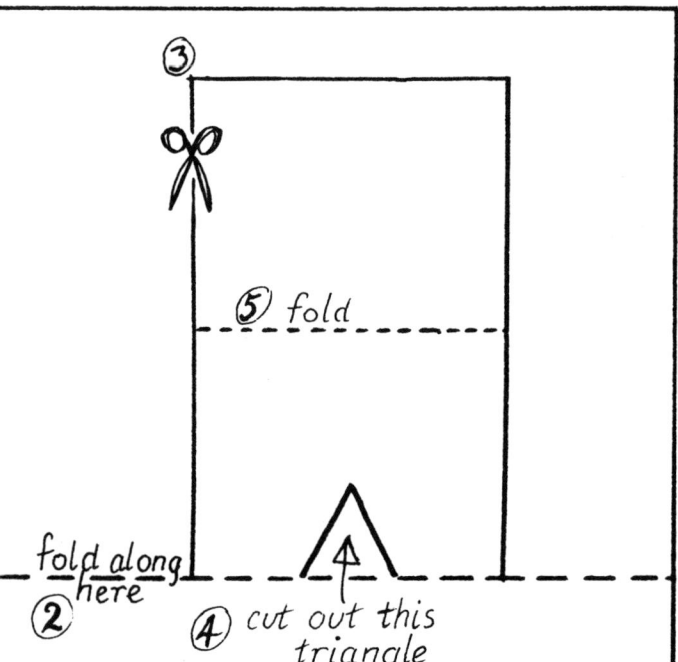

③
⑤ fold
fold along here
②
④ cut out this triangle

Fold the squeaker to look like this.

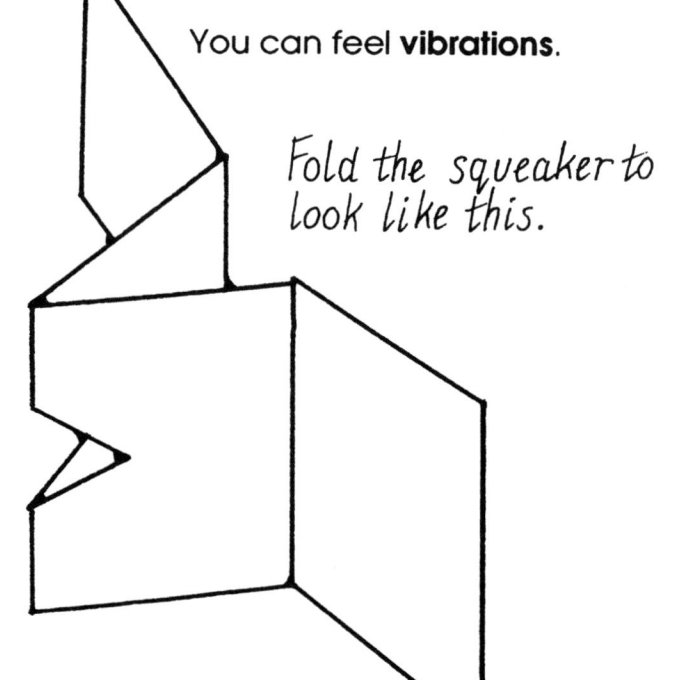

You can colour it.

CAT AND MOUSE

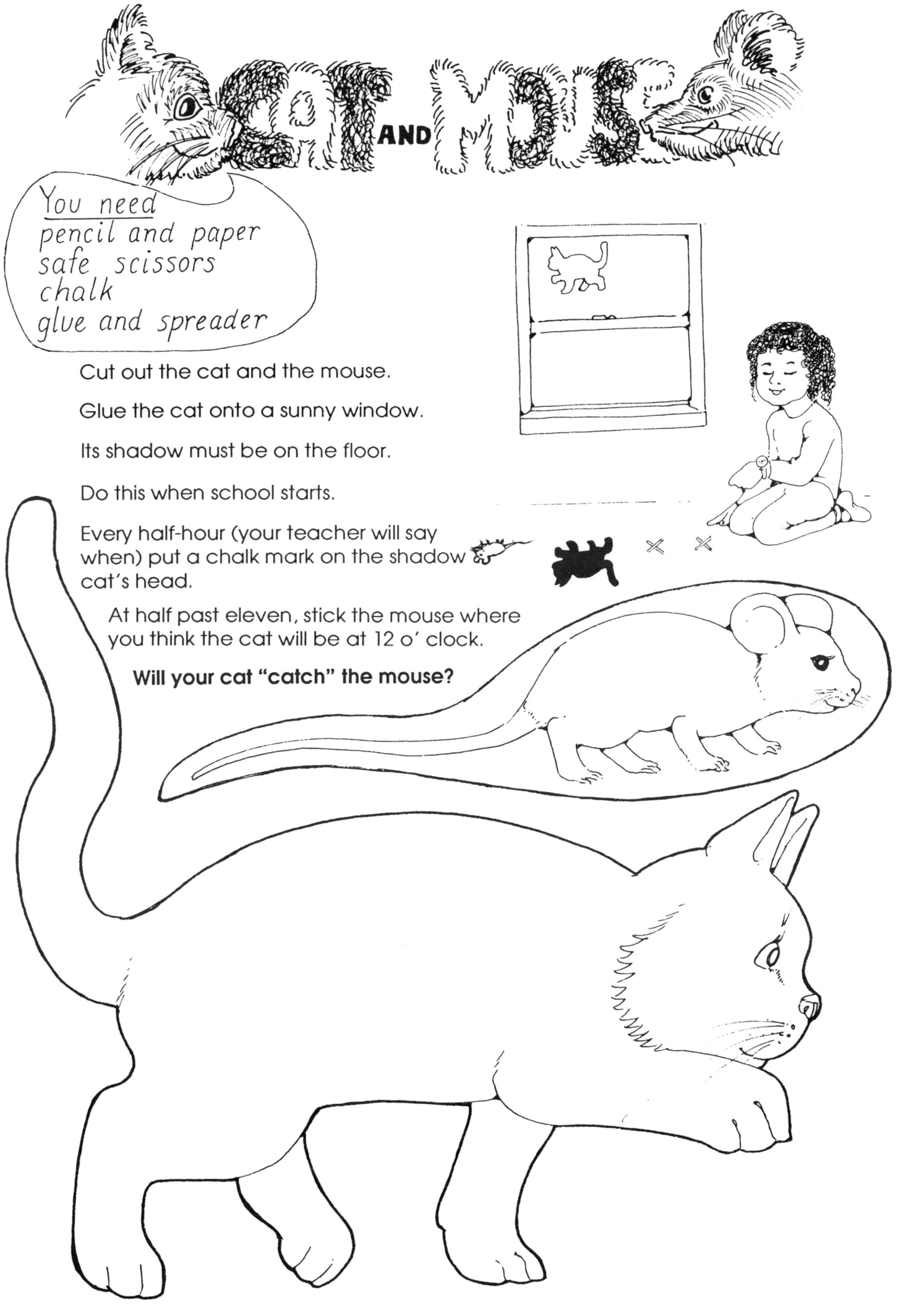

You need
pencil and paper
safe scissors
chalk
glue and spreader

Cut out the cat and the mouse.

Glue the cat onto a sunny window.

Its shadow must be on the floor.

Do this when school starts.

Every half-hour (your teacher will say when) put a chalk mark on the shadow cat's head.

At half past eleven, stick the mouse where you think the cat will be at 12 o' clock.

Will your cat "catch" the mouse?

This page may be photocopied for classroom use only

PLANET EARTH

You need
pencil and paper
crayons

You live on a planet called Earth.

It is shaped like a huge ball, floating in space.

Imagine that you can see Earth from
a spacecraft far out in space.

Draw and colour the spacecraft.

MATHS

Brain Waves offers a set of versatile, ready to use, ideas for mathematices teaching. They provide a wide range of supplementary activities to reinforce and consolidate previous work in a new and creative way. An investigative approach to mathematics is encouraged. Many of the activities are designed for group work thus encouraging mathematical communication skills and developing the social skills associated with the playing of games.

Brain Waves provides a source of instant lesson ideas for the harassed class teacher, supply teachers and all those required to take a class at a moment's notice.

SHEETS REQUIRING PREPARATION.

Funny Faces.	Cutting of the cards required. Colouring activity possible.
The Gingerbread	Cutting out required (mounting on card recommended).
Man Game.	Die required to play the game.
Variations.	Cutting out of different size bear shapes required. Could be developed into investigation of different sizes of the same type of object in the classroom e.g. pencils, bags, children. Introduce the idea of rank order.
Number Jig-Saw.	Cutting out of simple jigsaw pieces required.
Turn the Card.	Cut out domino cards provided and write the number symbol on the reverse side. One set of cards per group.
Count a Caterpillar.	Cutting out (and mounting on card) required. One set per player.

FUNNY FACES

Funny Faces is a matching game for young children

- Cut out the face squares so that there are 12 separate half faces.

- Shuffle them on the table.

- The children then match up the corresponding sides of the faces. These can be glued and mounted onto card to give longer life. Older children can draw on a body with arms and legs – from a funny face to a funny figure.

TEACHERS PAGE

THE GINGERBREAD MAN GAME

AIM: To reinforce number recognition 1 to 6

NUMBER OF PLAYERS: 2 to 6

WHAT YOU NEED: A master body for each player divided into parts and numbered 1 to 6 with a corresponding set of individual body parts numbered on one side. All of the above items are made from card.

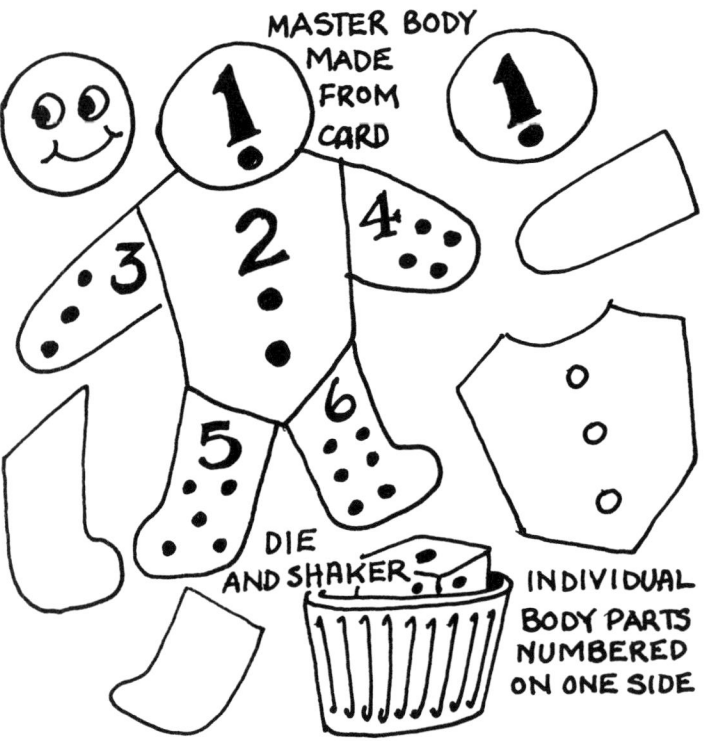

MASTER BODY MADE FROM CARD

DIE AND SHAKER

INDIVIDUAL BODY PARTS NUMBERED ON ONE SIDE

HOW TO PLAY:

• Each player has a master body and a set of corresponding body parts laid on the table with the numbered side facing up.

• Players take it in turns to throw the die.

• As the player throws a number she matches the correct part to place on the master body with numbered side down. GRADUALLY BUILDING UP THE GINGERBREAD MAN.

• If the player has already collected the part but throws the same number again she does nothing. The next player takes his turn.

• The first player with a completed Gingerbread Man is the winner.

TEACHERS PAGE

MASTER BODY OF THE GINGERBREAD MAN TO BE COPIED ON TO CARD AND CUT OUT.

VARIATIONS

The same principle can be adapted to make other games using favourite characters or animals.

DB DADDY BEAR

MB MUMMY BEAR

BB BABY BEAR

FOR EXAMPLE :

The three bears to incorporate the idea of size.

Mix up the body parts so that the child who is building up "Daddy Bear" has to pick out the "big" parts as well as the correct number. A game for 3 players.

TEACHERS PAGE

Daddy Bear, Mummy Bear and Baby Bear

Here are templates that you may use with your class.

Self Correcting Games

NUMBER JIGSAW

AIM: To recognise and match the number of objects to the numeral.

NUMBER OF PLAYERS: One

WHAT YOU NEED: A set of jigsaws - 1 piece number matching piece 1 - 10

HOW TO PLAY: The player matches the numeral to the correct piece if the jigsaw fits.

Later the child can put them in order.

1
2
3
5
TEACHERS PAGE

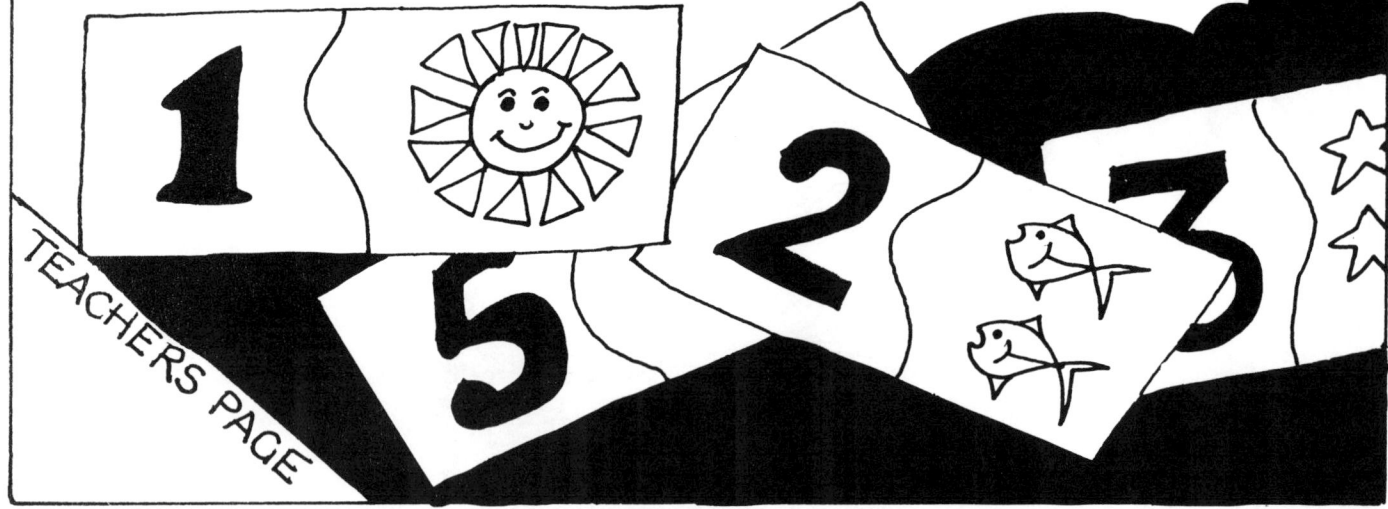

This page may be photocopied for classroom use only

TURN THE CARD

AIM: To learn number symbols

NUMBER OF PLAYERS: 2 or more

WHAT YOU NEED: A set of cards numbered 1 - 10, and on the reverse side the corresponding number of spots.

HOW TO PLAY: Place the cards in the middle of the table in a pile with the numbers facing up. The player looks at the symbol and can take a guess at the number. The player that makes the guess turns the card and checks the answer by counting the spots. If the player was correct he keeps the card. The player with the most cards at the end is the winner.

VARIATION: NUMBER SNAP

NUMBER OF PLAYERS: 2

WHAT YOU NEED: A set of cards per group of 2 children with number symbols 1 to 10.
A set of cards per group of two children marked with spots 1 to 10.

Each player has a set of cards of either symbols or spots. They shuffle the cards and lay the cards down face up, If the numeral and spots match the first player to shout "SNAP" wins the cards.

TEACHERS PAGE

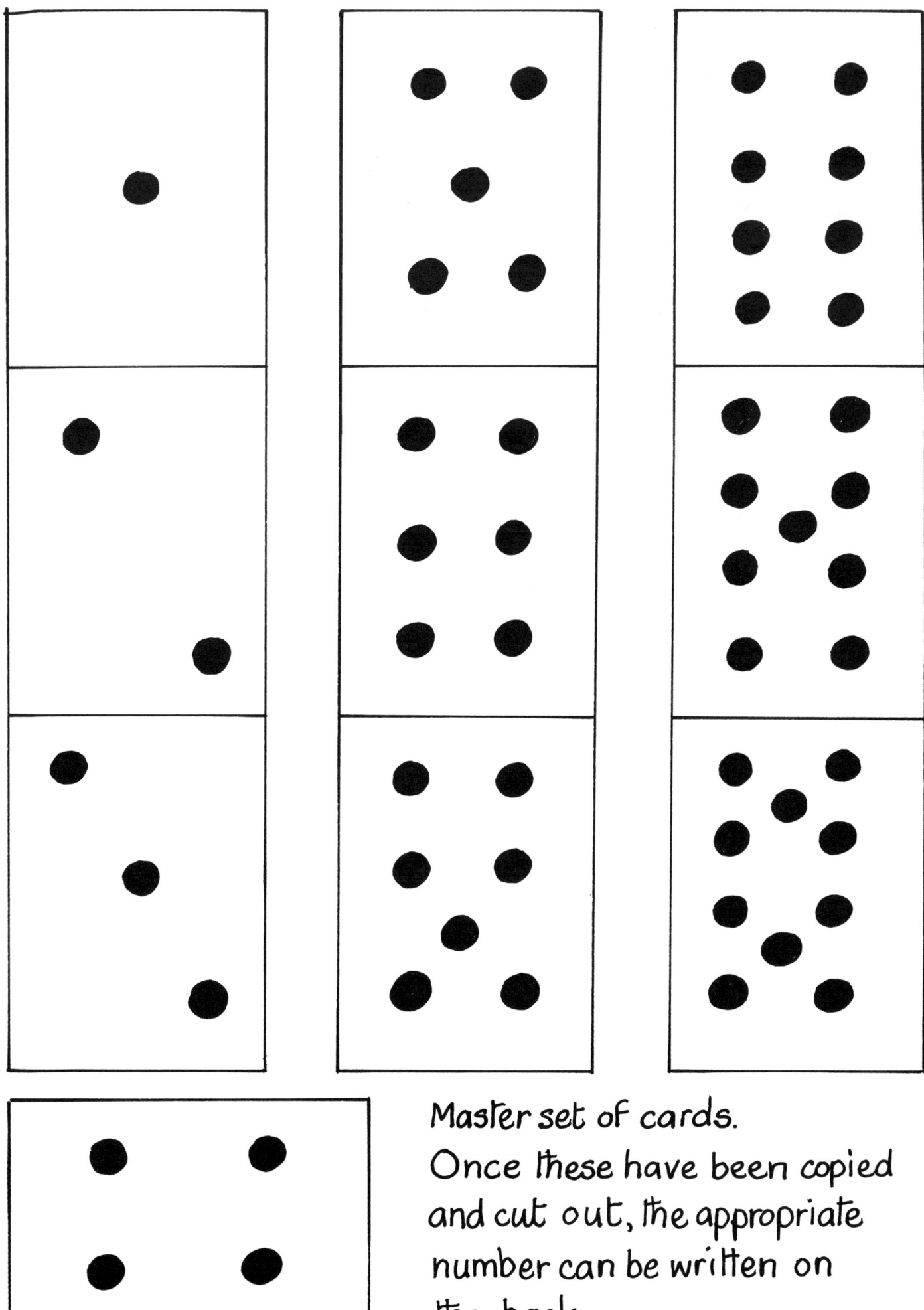

Master set of cards.
Once these have been copied
and cut out, the appropriate
number can be written on
the back.

COUNT A CATERPILLAR

AIM : A sorting game to give practise in sequencing numbers.

NUMBER OF PLAYERS : 2 to 4 players.

WHAT YOU NEED: 4 sets of cards with 10 cards per set, numbered 1 to 10. A set of cards are provided for photocopying.

(1) (2) (3) (4) (5) (6) (7) (8) (9) (10)

HOW TO PLAY: Place all the circles face down.
Take it in turn to pick up a circle.
Make a caterpillar by collecting the numbers 1 to 10.
Take it in turns to pick up one circle at a time.
If the circle has already been collected return the circle face down to the main group.
The first player to collect all 10 circles and put them in order is the winner.

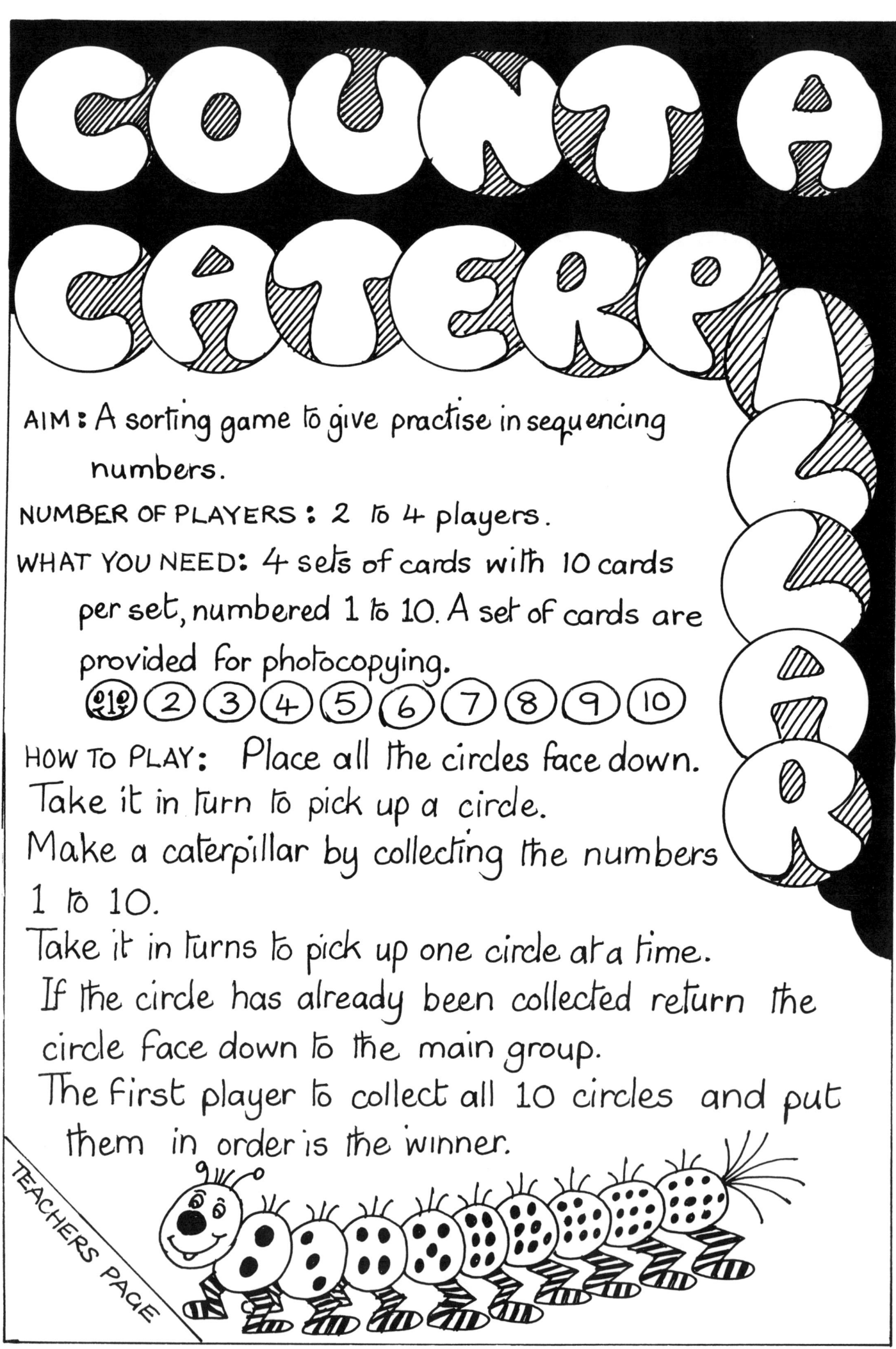

TEACHERS PAGE

A set of cards to be photocopied for the Caterpillar in "Count the Caterpillar."

ANIMAL MAGIC

Join the dots to see what animal you can make.

NAME_ _ _ _ _ _ _ _ _ _ _ _ _ _ _ _ _ CLASS_ _ _ _ _ _ _

TECHNOLOGY

Brain Waves Designing and Making aims to help teachers to recognise the potential for designing and making activities within their current classroom practice. Design problems should arise naturally out of pupils' classroom experience and can extend and enrich on-going work. Many curriculum areas provide contexts for design work. It may be that only a slight change of emphasis is required to provide a rich source of starting points for problem-solving activity. Once potential learning situations have been identified it is then a matter of how the task is presented, how the problems are posed and the style of the questions asked.

DESIGNING AND MAKING ..... not simply a matter of the finished product?

The process pupils go through when they proceed from problem to solution is the essence of designing and making. Pupils will observe, identify needs, research, plan, make, test, evaluate and modify.
The design process has traditionally been represented by a design 'loop'.

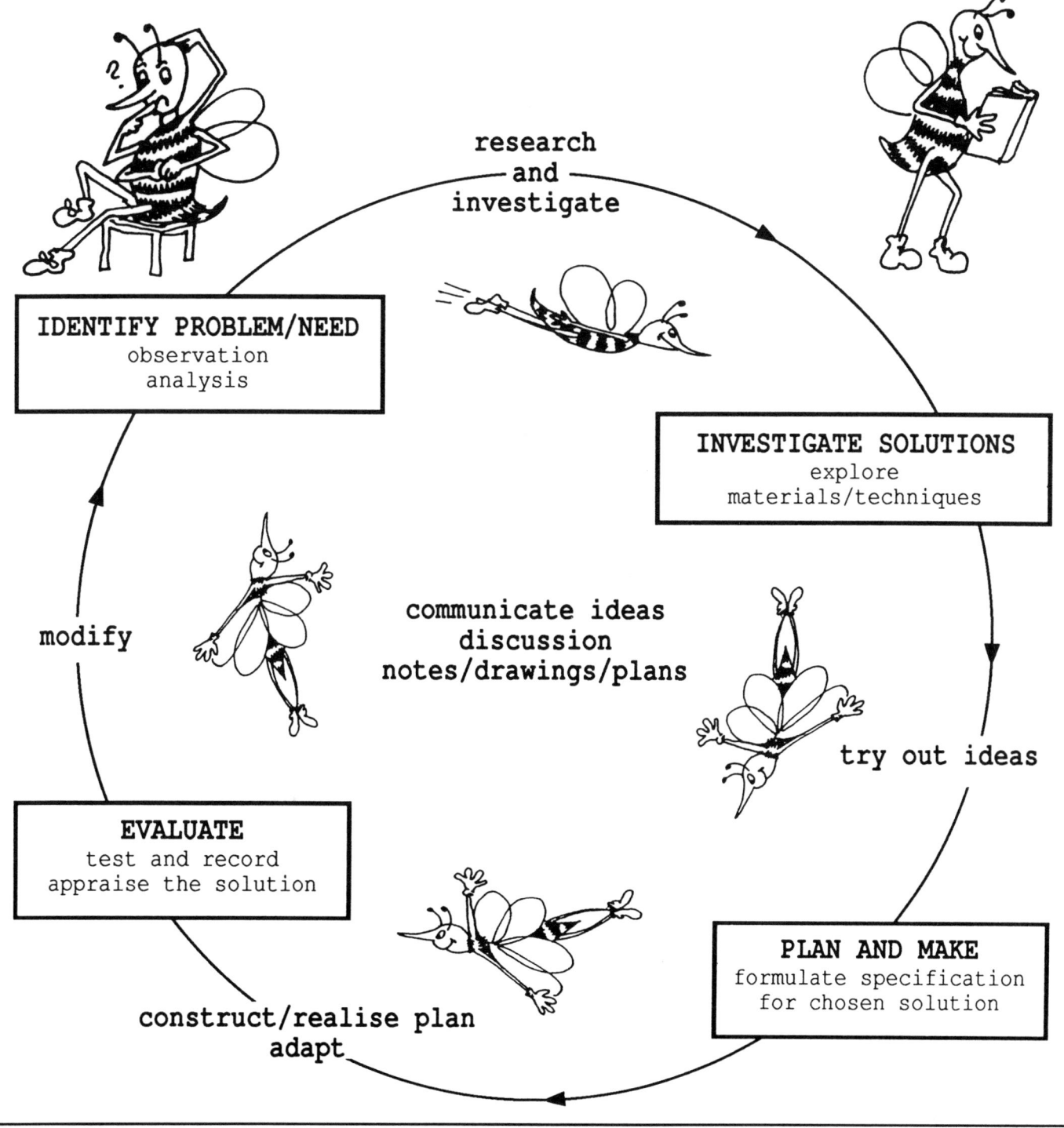

research
and
investigate

IDENTIFY PROBLEM/NEED
observation
analysis

INVESTIGATE SOLUTIONS
explore
materials/techniques

modify

communicate ideas
discussion
notes/drawings/plans

try out ideas

EVALUATE
test and record
appraise the solution

construct/realise plan
adapt

PLAN AND MAKE
formulate specification
for chosen solution

STARTING POINTS.....
An 'observation' walk in the locality to sketch the different shapes and construction of homes and buildings . . . . focus discussion on roof shapes . . . Book research to find out about shelter (through the ages and around the world) . . . Investigation of materials . . . which will keep out the rain? . . . Classification of materials (waterproof/non-waterproof) . . .

MATERIALS

newspaper (can be rolled to make strong supports)
plastic bags
adhesive tape
string
plastic hoops

(limited materials will 'focus' the design options)

THINGS TO THINK ABOUT

How can a sheet of newspaper be turned into a strong support?

How can the newspaper supports be joined together to make a strong frame?

How will the roof material be attached to the frame?

PREPARATION/EQUIPMENT/OTHER RESOURCES

Collection of visual stimulus material - roof shapes, tents etc.

Variety of materials for waterproof testing

Teddy bears!

MORE THINGS TO THINK ABOUT

How can the designs be tested fairly?

Are they waterproof?

Are they strong enough to stand up to the wind?

SKILLS TO BE DEVELOPED

Investigational . . .

Observation and classification of types of shelter. Testing of materials for waterproof qualities. Exploration of suitable structures

Practical . . .

Rolling and fixing supports
Assembly of structure

WHAT HAVE YOU DISCOVERED?

Which house is the most stable? Why?

Which frame shape is the strongest? Why?

Which house kept Teddy dry for the longest time? Why?

Teddy Bear

Poor Teddy is feeling very wet. He's been left outside in the rain. He would much rather be inside and dry.

DESIGN AND MAKE
a house to keep Teddy dry, using only the materials available.

THINK ABOUT— How could you make weak materials stronger?

THINK ABOUT— Will your design stand up to the wind as well?

STARTING POINTS......
Dragon stories and poems . . . discussion of pictures of dragons from fairy stories . . . research and comparison with Chinese dragons . . . identification of dragon features . . . encourage pencil drawings . . . focus discussion on parts which could move . . . classification of types of movement (up and down/in and out/round and round etc.)

MATERIALS

card
corrugated card
junk materials e.g. boxes, card tubes, plastic pots, lollipop sticks.
thin dowelling
wire
paper fasteners
string
materials for decoration (coloured tissue, sequins, feathers etc.)

THINGS TO THINK ABOUT

Which part of the dragon will move? eyes? jaws? wings? tongue? tail? head?

How will you make the part move? by pulling a string? by turning a wheel? with a lever?

PREPARATION/EQUIPMENT/OTHER RESOURCES

Collection of visual stimulus material
Stories and poems.
Cutting and measuring equipment.

Skill card nos. 1,2 and 6

MORE THINGS TO THINK ABOUT

How could the dragon be made to move along the floor?

How could wheels be attached?

How will you decorate and finish the dragon? Will it be friendly or fierce?

SKILLS TO BE DEVELOPED

Investigational . . .

Observation and recording of dragon features. Hypothesis and testing of movement mechanisms.

Practical . . .

drawing, measuring, marking, cutting, shaping, forming, construction and assembly.

WHAT HAVE YOU DISCOVERED?

Which movement mechanisms were most successful? Why?

Could you use these ideas for movement in other situations?

Which design looks most fierce? Why?

DRAGONS

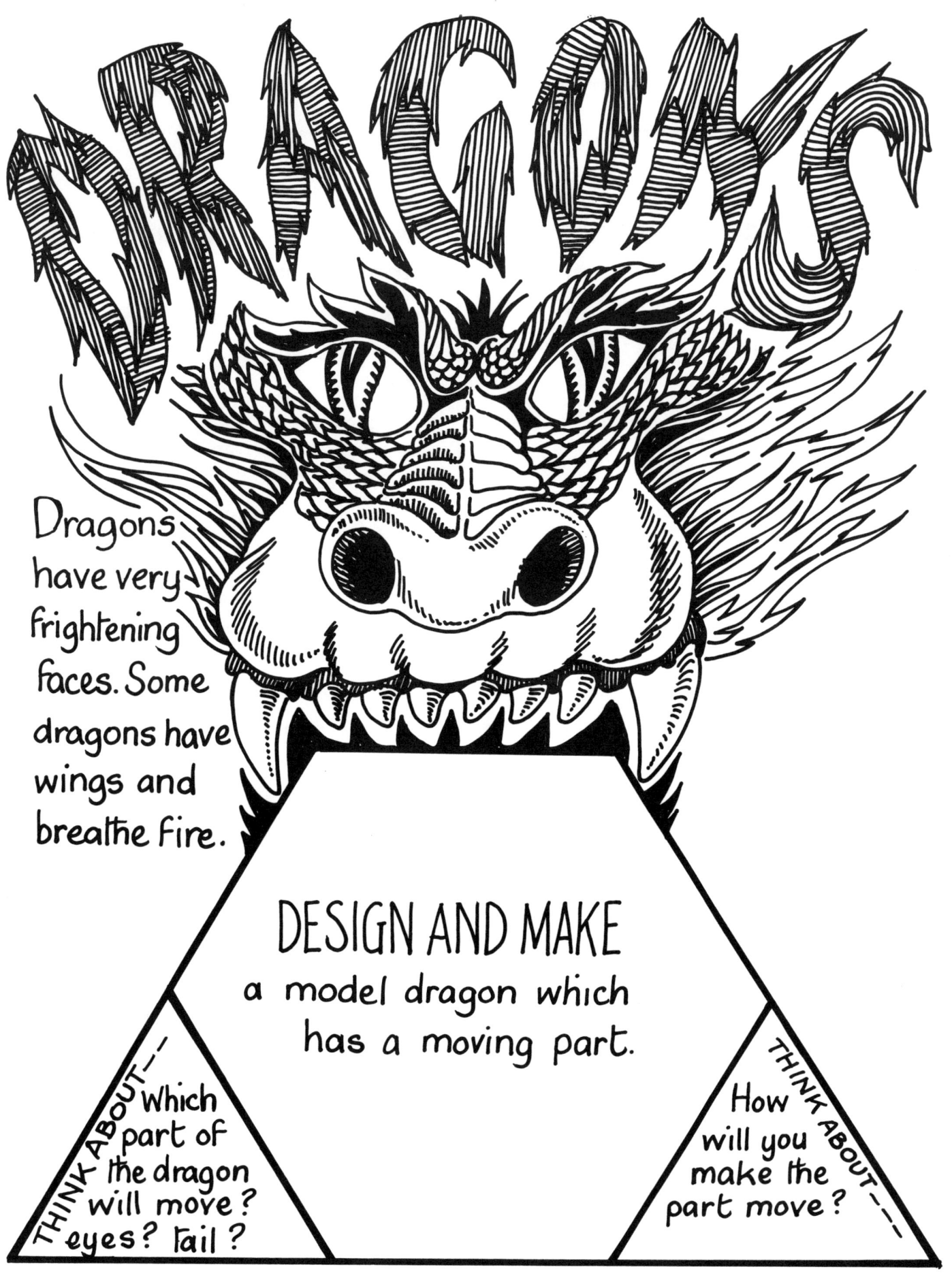

Dragons have very frightening faces. Some dragons have wings and breathe fire.

DESIGN AND MAKE
a model dragon which has a moving part.

THINK ABOUT — Which part of the dragon will move? eyes? tail?

THINK ABOUT — How will you make the part move?

STARTING POINTS . . . .

A study of children's first books for ideas, paying particular attention to colour and simplicity of design . . . focus on safety (the mobile must be secure!) . . . investigate ways of making sounds (rustling tin foil, wind chimes etc.) . . .

MATERIALS

wire coat hangers
art straws
dowelling
wire, string, fishing line
adhesive tape
junk materials eg. small containers,
card tubes, bottle tops
card (various thicknesses)
felt
tin foil
clay (to make wind chimes)

THINGS TO THINK ABOUT

How will you balance the mobile?

Think about the weight of the mobile objects.

What safety factors will you need to consider? (Remember that the mobile will hang above the baby.)

Will colour be important?

PREPARATION/EQUIPMENT/OTHER RESOURCES

Children's books for design ideas.

Examples of existing mobile designs.

Safety knives and rulers

Skill card no. 5

MORE THINGS TO THINK ABOUT

Could the mobile make a sound as it moves?

What will make the noise?

Test your designs.

Do they attract a baby's attention?

SKILLS TO BE DEVELOPED

Investigational . . .

Research and evaluation of children's books for design ideas. Hypothesis and testing of mobile designs

Practical . . .

Measuring, marking, cutting, joining and fixing, framework assembly.

WHAT HAVE YOU DISCOVERED?

Which mobile makes the most attractive display? Why?

Which mobile moves most freely? Why?

Which mobile makes the most attractive sound? How?

How could you improve you design?

Moving Shapes

New born babies will focus on brightly coloured objects that move.

If this baby had something attractive to look at while lying in its cot it might not cry so much!

ah-ah-ah! ah-ah-ah! ah-ah-ah!
ah-ah ah-ah

DESIGN AND MAKE a free moving mobile to hang over a baby's cot and attract its attention.

THINK ABOUT—
How will the mobile move freely?

THINK ABOUT—
How will you balance the different mobile objects?

STARTING POINTS . . . . . . Dance and drama activities . . . .
exploration of bodily movements, joints etc. . . . Animation and development of a
favourite story . . . . . . Religious and moral themes (good/bad) . . . Emotions
(happiness/sadness/fear/jealousy etc). The 'focus' of the task may concentrate on
movement or character or both.

MATERIALS

(according to 'focus' of task)
card
paper
paper fasteners
string/wire/fishing line
junk materials e.g. cotton reels,
card tubes, lollipop sticks
scrap fabrics and wool
polystyrene balls
thin dowelling
adhesive.

THINGS TO THINK ABOUT

Which parts of your body bend?

How can you make a joint for the
puppet?

How will you operate the joint?

PREPARATION/EQUIPEMNT/OTHER RESOURCES

Visit to school by professional
puppeteer.

Collection of puppets eg. string,
glove, sock and finger puppets.

Reference books on puppet making
A skeleton or skeleton diagram
safely knives and rulers

Skill card no. 6

MORE THNGS TO THINK ABOUT

What sort of character will your
puppet play? happy? sad? angry?

How can you show their character?

Will the puppets speak?

SKILLS TO BE DEVELOPED

Investigational . . .

Observation and analysis of body
movements and/or facial expressions.
Hypothesis and testing of movement
mechanisms

Practical . . .

Measuring, marking, cutting, joining
and fixing. Operation of puppet.

WHAT HAVE YOU DISCOVERED?

Which is the easiest way to operate
the puppet?

How could you improve your design?

PULL THE OTHER ONE

Puppets bring a story to life. Create a main character to animate a story.

DESIGN AND MAKE
a puppet with at least one moving part. Your design must only use the materials provided.

THINK ABOUT Which parts of the puppet will move?

THINK ABOUT How to make the puppet easy to operate?

STARTING POINTS . . . .

An investigation into different methods of storing and carrying collections of everyday items in the home and at school (sewing boxes, cleaning equipment, tools etc.) . . . Focus on desk items . . . demonstration and discussion of the problems associated with the storage of many small items in one container eg. plastic ice cream container with tangled elastic bands, paper clips etc..... Analysis of the different sizes, shapes and weights of the items to be stored.

MATERIALS

junk materials eg. cardboard tubes, boxes, plastic containers
stiff card
corrugated card
corruflute
adhesives
(wood)

THINGS TO THINK ABOUT

Will you need a labelling system?

Will the system be easy to use or is it complicated?

Will it encourage tidiness?

How will you make it stable?

PREPARATION/EQUIPMENT/OTHER RESOURCES

Display/collection of different storage systems.

Catalogues and magazines advertising storage systems.

Equipment for cutting card and plastic (wood)

MORE THINGS TO THINK ABOUT

Is the container easy to move from one place to another?

How could you make your design personal?

How will your design be "finished off"?

SKILLS TO BE DEVELOPED

Investigational . . .

Classification of items to be stored.
Analysis of requirements.
Exploration of suitable materials and techniques for construction

Practical . . .

marking, measuring, cutting, forming, shaping, assembly.

WHAT HAVE YOU DISCOVERED?

Which design is the easiest to use? Why?

Which design is the most stable? Why?

Which design is the most portable? Why?

Does your container stay tidy over a period of time?

KEEP IT TIDY!

Now, where is it? It was here a few minutes ago....----

Paul can never find his pens, pencils, ruler, rubbers, paper clips or anything else as his desk is always in a mess. Is yours?

DESIGN AND MAKE

a container for pens, pencils, rulers, rubbers, paperclips etc. so that they can be found easily. The container should be designed to stand on a desk but be portable as well.

THINK ABOUT---- How many pens, pencils, rulers etc. will have to be stored?

THINK ABOUT---- How will the size, shape and weight of the items affect your design?

STARTING POINTS

...... A study of how and where birds feed . . . book research into differnt types of birds and their feeding habits . . . . wildlife videos . . . . a visit to a bird sanctuary . . . writing letters to the RSPB for information . . . . discussion and design of a survey chart to complete during a bird watching session in the school grounds . . . encourage sketches of the birds observed

MATERIALS

junk materials e.g. plastic cartons, trays, bottles etc.
Wood (various thicknesses)
cm^2 wood and dowelling
wire
chicken wire
string
corruflute
adhesive
elastic bands
nails

THINGS TO THINK ABOUT

What sort of food will you use to feed the birds?

How will you keep the food inside the feeder?

How will the birds be able to reach the food ? (Think about the different positions birds feed in)

PREPARATION/EQUIPMENT/OTHER RESOURCES

Arrange video recordings

Send for RSPB information pack

Arrange visiting speaker

Cutting tools and other wood working equipment (to be used under supervision)
Sandpaper and varnish

MORE THINGS TO THINK ABOUT

How could you control the amount of food which is dispensed?

How could your design influence the types of bird attracted to the feeder?

Could you include a method to indicate when the feeder is empty?

SKILLS TO BE DEVELOPED

Investigational. . .

Information and study skills.
Observation and recording of bird behaviour. Interpretation of findings. Hypothesis and testing of bird feeder design and its position.

Practical . . .

Measuring, marking, cutting, forming, joining and fixing.

WHAT HAVE YOU DISCOVERED?

Where do different species of birds prefer to feed?

What do different birds prefer to eat?

Which design attracted the most birds? Why?

Which was the best position for your feeder?

This page may be photocopied for classroom use only

STARTING POINTS . . . . . .

A survey of hobbies interests and pastimes enjoyed by members of the class . . . An investigation of symbols and logos (roadsigns, sports club badges, brownie and cub badges etc) . . . . .

MATERIALS

Card (various thicknesses)
paper
paper fasteners
adhesive tape
glue
safety pins
materials for decoration

THINGS TO THINK ABOUT

Do badges always have to be round?

What other shapes could be used?

What symbols are usually used to represent your interest?

Can you think of something more unusual?

PREPARATION/EQUIPMENT/OTHER RESOURCES

Collection of examples of symbols and logos used to represnt ideas eg. travel brochures, Highway Code, Olympic games, hobbies magazines etc.

Shape templates

Safety knives and rulers

Skill card nos. 1, 2 and 6

MORE THINGS TO THINK ABOUT

Could you make the badge more interesting by including a moving part?
a foot kicking a ball?
waves on the water?
a book which opens?
a dog with a wagging tail?

SKILLS TO BE DEVELOPED

Investigational . . .

Observation and analyisis of symbolic representation of ideas.
Exploration of suitable symbols to represent hobbies

Practical . . .
marking, measuring, cutting, joining and fixing.

WHAT HAVE YOU DISCOVERED?

Does your badge tell others what your interests are?

Can they tell immediately or do they have to guess?

How could you make the badge clearer?

BADGE BRIGADE

Why do people wear badges?

Who wears badges?

What do badges tell us?

DESIGN AND MAKE a big badge to show what your main hobby or interest is.

Your design must not use words. It could have a moving part.

THINK ABOUT — Will your design be clear to understand from a distance?

THINK ABOUT — What symbols could you use to represent your hobby?

HINGES AND PIVOTS

Hinges to open and close

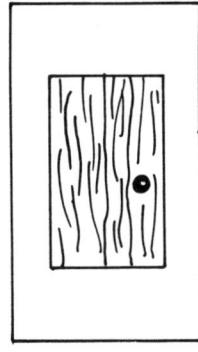

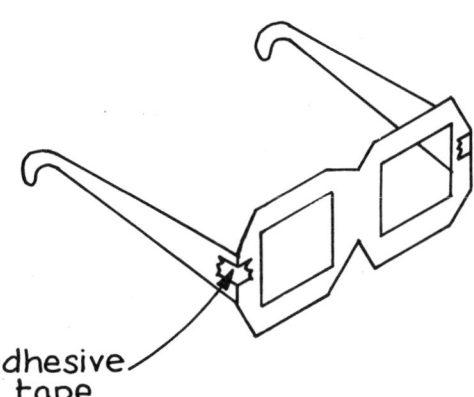

adhesive tape

Hinges to change a message

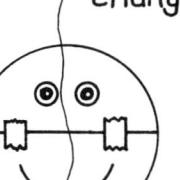

pull string to change expression

draw a sad face on a card circle

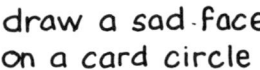

draw a happy smile on a half circle.

Stick onto sad face with tape

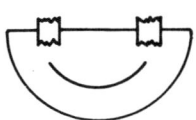

PROBLEM TO SOLVE: What do you draw on the other side?

Pivots for movement

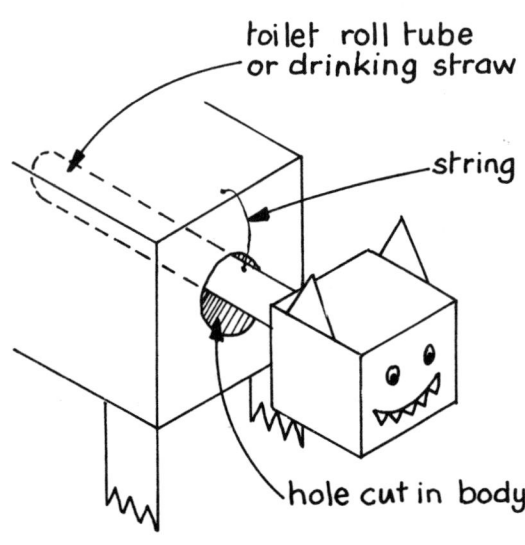

toilet roll tube or drinking straw

string

hole cut in body

paper fastener pivots

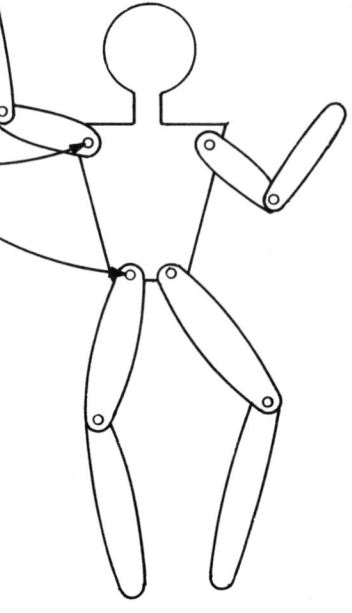

PROBLEM TO SOLVE: How can you make the head balance?

HINT: Use a plasticine weight